A Memoir

A Memoir

John C. Foster, Sr.

INTERVIEW
You
Athens, Georgia

Published by Interview You, an imprint of Miglior Press, LLC
Athens, Georgia

www.interviewyou.net

ISBN: 978-0-9822726-6-4

First Edition

Printed in the United States of America

I dedicate this book to my wonderful wife, Bobbie Carpenter Foster, for loving me unconditionally, for always being there when I needed you, and for showing me how wonderful love can be when God gives you the right person.

Contents

Part I. My Life

Part II. Thoughts about Issues

Part III. Postscript

Part I

MY LIFE

1. Childhood

I was born and reared in Habersham County, Georgia. I was born on April 2, 1935, at the family home, located off old Cleveland Road, near where I currently live. I was born into a farm family. Both my parents were in the profession of farming, small farming as compared to the large-scale farming one observes in some states today. I attended Habersham County public schools, graduating from South Habersham High School in 1953. I was the first member of my family to graduate from college. However, it took me sixteen years, attending off and on, with military time in between, to get through college. I graduated from Piedmont College in 1969. I attended church, of course—Level Grove Baptist Church—where I first joined the church.

I came from a family with a very stable environment. I had great parents, but we were poor. I can still recall the day they first turned the electricity on at our farm. And to underscore the point, another one of the most exciting things that happened in our family was when my dad bought a manure spreader. We had always spread the manure from the barns by hand, and we thought that the spreader was a really exciting, miraculous invention.

We never owned a car. My parents did buy a truck at one point, but our mode of transportation when I was very young was a mule and wagon. I know that might sound unreal today, but it is true.

I was the second person in our family to graduate from high school. My older brother, of course, preceded me and graduated first. I was basically an average student in high school. I didn't make straight A's—I made a few occasionally—but I was just an average, typical student who had to work on the farm after school. And this consequently hindered me from participating in a lot of extracurricular activities as far as school was concerned. However, I did participate in football and 4-H.

My father was one of the first farmers who got into the production of growing chickens commercially. I remember when we built our first chicken house. It probably was about 50 feet long, and we thought that was a pretty big building at that time. We mainly raised hens and commercial eggs; we never invested in what are called broilers today.

That was the basic way we made our living, but we also always had a good garden. My father never really liked to grow row crops, for example, we never grew cotton, but we grew hay, and we grew corn, primarily for making corn meal. We had corn meal ground for us and also for feeding the animals. We slaughtered our own animals for consumption purposes. My father would kill at least five big hogs a year, a byproduct of which was tubs and tubs of lard. He would hang the meat in an old smokehouse and salt it. How it would keep so well, I don't know, but it would. And we would occasionally kill our own beef.

But even though we were very poor financially, we were very rich as far as our family environment was concerned. I thought as I was growing up that having to eat gravy and biscuits, and taking a biscuit-and-ham sandwich to school for lunch was a very embarrassing situation. At that time I always wondered why I couldn't have a sandwich out of loaf bread, but we didn't have loaf bread. But when I was older, I realized that the friends I referred to as my city friends always had the loaf bread, and I had the biscuits. But they always wished that they had the biscuits, and I wished I had the loaf bread. So it's just a matter of perception on the part of everybody concerned.

I also grew up having to eat fried chicken for breakfast. Nobody had more marvelous meals! And I never missed a meal. My mother would cook three great meals every day.

Also, my mother made our clothes out of chicken-feed sacks.

John C. Foster, Sr.

Every shirt I had as a boy was homemade, and I never had a suit. Even when I graduated from high school, I did not have a suit. I had to borrow a sport coat from my older brother to wear to graduation.

I remember that we would go to church every Sunday. We always walked to church, both there and back, until later on when my parents got a big truck. I had to wear either overalls or just a pair of khaki pants; I didn't have any dress pants. One day a friend and I were walking back home from church, and I was admiring his really pretty pair of dress pants. I told him that I wished I had a pair of dress pants. He said, "Well, we're both about the same size; I'll tell you what we'll do. Let's just swap pants." So that's how I obtained my first pair of dress pants. We just traded pants right there in the middle of the road.

I did a lot of interesting things growing up. We kept ourselves occupied as youngsters by playing games like cow-pasture football or cow-pasture baseball. One of the most popular and fun things to do on a Sunday afternoon was to go out into the woods and swing from tree to tree. How we survived all that without getting killed or breaking bones, I don't know, but we did it. Sometimes on a winter day, if we had a nice snow, we would go out and run rabbits down, physically run them down. That was fun. We would also trap rabbits and squirrels. We would dress them and bring them into town and trade them for some candy at the store. The folks in town liked the fact that the rabbits and squirrels were already dressed, so all they had to do was take them home and cook them.

We did other typical things that youngsters did back then. For example, we had a team of goats that we used to pull us in a wagon. It was just a small wagon, but it was sufficient and that was a fun thing to do. We could always find fun things to do, but never would we wander around trying to find trouble.

If we didn't have something to do, my father had a knack for finding something that we needed to be doing. Many a rainy day, when I thought we ought to be relaxing and doing nothing,

I would be sent along with my brothers to the corn crib to shuck corn so that we'd have plenty of corn shucked for the hogs and for corn meal.

It seems to me that the type of life that I lived as a child has largely disappeared, but I had a typical rural rearing for that time.

2. 4-H

I think one of the interesting things about my life is how I managed to end up in a business situation even though I came from an environment of financial poverty. I was very bashful, and even backward in some ways. But when I was in school, I took an interest in 4-H, and the county agent took an interest in me. Fortunately, I succeeded in 4-H and became an officer and, ultimately, even the president of the 4-H club. I could win those elections. Back then I never really gave that much thought. But yet when I look back at it, it was during those young years in 4-H, and to some degree FFA, that I developed some of my leadership skills.

I thought that I was a terrible speaker. (I've always been my worst critic.) But I remember once being asked to give a demonstration at the University of Georgia on the process of planting a pine tree, and I agreed. I developed my kit for demonstrating the process. With the help of the county agent and his secretary, I wrote four typewritten pages of material that I memorized to use in my demonstration. The county agent invited all of us that were involved in giving demonstrations or presenting projects at the university to his home to practice our presentations.

So I went, of course, and at some point it was my turn to speak. The audience was very small, about a dozen in all. I began my demonstration, and all of a sudden I forgot what I had practiced to say. I got through about the first page of what I had memorized, but then my mind went blank. I went totally blank, and then I became just petrified. I threw my props down and ran. I was humiliated, so embarrassed that I had forgotten my part. As I look back, I know it was unnecessary for me to run, but at the time I was just so embarrassed.

The county agent chased me down, talked to me, and told me he wanted me to come back. He said, "John, you're going to do this. You can do it. I'm going to work with you."

I'll always be indebted to him for that. I went back, and I did my demonstration. It was still a struggle, but I managed to do it. Later I went down to the university and successfully gave my presentation. I didn't win first place, but I did place.

That whole experience was a powerful one. It hurt, and I still remember that moment of petrification. In later years when I would be giving a speech, sometimes that moment would flash in my mind and would almost petrify me again. But the experience also strengthened me and showed me that I really could do whatever I set out to do. It was an important lesson for me, and I think it's what helped me to grow into the role of leadership positions.

In college I never really got involved in leadership because I didn't have time. I was married and had children. In fact, both of my sons attended my college graduation.

My experience in leadership all started with my early years in 4-H.

3. Early Jobs

I enjoyed listening to the radio as a youngster, but owning a radio station was never in my dreams. My ultimate dream was to be a chief radio announcer. I guess, really, my wildest dream was to get any kind of job at a radio station.

When radio station WCON was being built in Cornelia, I was a student at South Habersham High School. I wanted a job as I had never held a real job. I really wanted a job as a disc jockey with the station, and I made several visits to the guy who was building the station, seeking employment and an opportunity to learn, to be trained. I had a difficult time convincing him that I was capable. After all, I had no background in radio. And frankly, I don't know anybody today who is as bad as I was then. I think I finally got the owner's attention because of my determination: I kept going there, checking to see if maybe he had a little job for me, something that would open the door for me to be a radio announcer. I had nighttime work in mind because I had to go to school during the day.

Finally, my repeated visits brought an offer. One day as I was visiting with him again, I asked him if he had a job for me. "Yeah," he said, "I've got a job I'll let you do. You can dig the septic tank hole."

"I'll do it," I said. And I did it. My psychology was that I'll do anything for this opportunity. And that attitude paid off for me. Soon afterwards, the owner let me audition to be an announcer. I did my audition at the station in Gainesville, and I thought I was just horrible. However, the guy that was doing the recording thought that I might have some potential as an announcer. He told the owner, "I'd give him a try if I were you." So he did. I started out working for him on night shift, seven days a week.

He finally told me that I had to take a day off, that I had to stay away for one day.

Pay was not even a factor for me then; it was the opportunity that interested me. At that time my goal was to become the chief radio announcer. I don't know if I ever met that goal, but I was finally working at a radio station. I was a radio announcer.

Working at the station was very interesting. Country music bands would come into the studio and play live on the air, and my favorite, gospel groups, would come in to the studio and play, too. We programmed a variety of different types of music, even classical. When I went on the board each evening, the first program I would have to handle was called "Sundown Serenade." It was classical music, and I hated it. I couldn't even pronounce the names of the artists. I'd have to seek help, and some of my friends, dear friends even to this day, helped me get the pronunciations at least nearly right.

But doing that show was a good thing for me because it taught me to appreciate classical music. In fact, today, classical music is one of my favorite forms of music. But, my interest in classical music really started one evening at the station when I was playing the "William Tell Overture." As I listened to it, I thought, "Gosh, I like that. That's good! Maybe if I'll just listen, I might learn to like some of this other music." And that's how I got started liking classical music.

After I graduated from high school, I tried to go to North Georgia College in Dahlonega, but I couldn't cut it over there. I didn't have any money, and I felt so inferior because I couldn't afford the nice things that the other students had. It was also very obvious to me that I was weak academically, and so I only attended for one quarter.

I came back to Habersham County and wanted something to do, so I applied to manage the Grand Theater. I'd never managed a theater or had anything to do with one, except that I did go to see movies. My parents allowed me to go. A friend would come and take my brother and me to the movies maybe once a week, or every other week, or something like that. I had fifty cents allowance. That fifty cents would buy me admission to the movie, and a milkshake, and a hot dog. I had a good time and a good meal for fifty cents.

Anyway, I got the job. The owner of the theater told me later on that he thought I had more brass than anybody he had ever seen, to come in and want to manage a theater when I didn't have any experience whatsoever, and no business background at all. But he told me that he wanted me to go to the Grand Theater in Cornelia, where I would be trained to manage the Clarkesville theater. So I did, and the man who trained me at the Cornelia theater told the owner of the theater company that he felt like I was capable of handling the Cornelia theater. So they turned the Grand Theater over to me, and I managed it for a year. I managed it very successfully. In fact, the last week I managed it, we made a comfortable profit, which was in those days a very good profit.

One of the things that I remember from that job is one of the movies that I showed toward the end of my career as manager of the theater. It was called "The Moon is Blue," and it was the first risqué movie that was produced in those days. It was widely popular throughout the country, so they booked it for Cornelia. It only had one line in it that was suggestive, but that line made the movie very popular, and I never will forget it: a couple is in the back seat of a car or a cab, and the woman looks over at the man and says, "You wouldn't try to seduce me, would you?" That was the only suggestive thing about the movie. My, how times have changed.

4. The Service

When I left my job at the theater, the Korean War was in progress. One day I was talking with the lady who ran the local draft board, and I asked her, "Are you going to draft me?"

"Yes," she said.

I asked her, "When am I going to be drafted?"

"In about two or three months, maybe a little longer," she said.

"Well, if you're going to draft me that soon, just go ahead and draft me now," I said.

When I popped off and said that, little did I believe that she would really do that. But she did, and I was drafted.

I spent two years in the military, which was probably one of the most enriching experiences of my life, outside of my academic experiences. I was trained as a combat soldier, a private, to go to Korea. However, the war at that time had apparently started slowing down. I didn't know it at the time, but I think our country was getting almost to the point of throwing in the towel.

Nevertheless, after we finished basic training at Fort Jackson, South Carolina, I was still destined to go to Korea. But one day as we were all standing at attention, they began calling out our assignments, and, to my surprise, my assignment turned out not to be Korea. My assignment was to go to Fort Riley, Kansas. There were only one or two others in my company that got different assignments; almost everyone else went to Korea. Why a few of us were picked not to go to Korea, I don't know. But I was sent to Fort Riley, Kansas, which is also where I concluded my military career.

John C. Foster, Sr.

At Fort Riley, I managed a regimental parts office or parts store. I'd never had any experience in that, but they put me in the parts department, and I was one of two or three managers. Each of us would manage the office part of the time; it was mostly give and take, depending on whoever was available to look after it at any given time.

Then, all of a sudden one day, they said that my company was going to Germany. They were going to send our whole company to Germany. But again to my surprise, for some strange reason I was not sent with the rest of my unit. When I asked the Captain why, he said, "I asked them to hold you here because you are managing our parts division, and I need you here." And I thought, "Well, that's fine with me."

But not long after that, my captain was transferred and left me there. And the next thing I know, I wound up being sent over to the main post at Fort Riley. As I only had a few months of enlistment left, they put me into a supply section of the company to help with supplies and with recruits in basic training. I despised that! I'd been through all that, and I did not want to be involved with it again.

Through the help of a friend, I finally managed to get myself transferred to another division within the main post at Fort Riley. When I arrived, the commander in charge wanted to know what I was doing there. My reply? "I don't know sir; I was just sent here."

He said, "Well, what can you do?" I told him what I could do, what I had been trained to do.

He said, "Well, go down to the motor pool and see if they can find something for you to do."

So, I did, and the guy there asked me if I could drive a bus.

I said, "Sure, I can drive a bus." Well, the truth was I *had* driven a school bus, but I had never driven a Greyhound-style bus.

Nevertheless, the guy said he'd try me out, so we got in a bus. I had observed these buses being driven by other soldiers, and I thought I could drive one, too. But when I made the first turn, I almost knocked down a sign, and the guy said, "You've never driven a bus like this; I can tell you that right now."

"Well, I have to admit that I have not driven this kind of bus before," I said.

Nevertheless, the guy said he thought they could train me, and so they took a day or two to do so. After that, I drove buses. I would drive a bus down to Manhattan, Kansas, pick up ROTC cadets and take them to Topeka. I did that for a while. Then I worked as a theater projectionist on weekends and at night. I worked in the theater that showed the movies for the generals and other high-ranking officers, which enabled me to make a lot of good friends.

When I look back over that period of time, I find myself asking, "Why did all this happen the way it did?" And I'm firmly convinced that it happened for this reason. It was when I was in the military that I, being a Baptist, made a decision that I would accept Christ. I think that was part of the Lord's plan.

You see, when I went to Kansas, I wanted to be active in church on the weekends, and I was, along with many other young soldiers. But the American Baptist church there was not particularly satisfying to a lot of us because we grew up as Southern Baptists. So a group of us decided to form our own church, and we did. We started out in a new-car showroom that had gone defunct, and in a matter of just a few months we had outgrown the showroom and built the first section of a new church building. It was made out of concrete blocks. It housed Sunday school rooms and a fellowship hall. Upon its completion, I was right at the end of my military career, and soon afterwards, I left Kansas. But the soldiers that remained, and those that followed continued to support that church. And today it is a fully developed church. It has a sanctuary and a complete array of facilities. 2004 marked its fiftieth anniversary.

Back then, I just figured maybe that's what the Lord had in mind for me, and that's the reason everything transpired as it did.

I didn't plan it. I didn't think about it. I never thought about it until one day when somebody asked me to come and speak in a church. That led me to revisit my life. And in doing so, I found that many of the things that had happened in my life seemed to have happened for a definite reason. They weren't really things that I had said, "This is the goal that I'm reaching for." They just happened. And I believe they happened for a purpose. To this day, I have maintained my strong faith in God and his will for my life.

5. Sandersville

One story that I think is interesting is how I, who had no money, managed to buy a radio station.

The fact is I had an uncle, H. L. Webster (married to my father's sister, Allie Ree), who had made quite a bit of money planting pine trees. In so doing, he invented a pine-tree planter, which added to his success by increasing the number of trees he could plant. This resulted in corporate and government contracts to set out trees. One day, out of the clear blue sky, he asked me, "How would you like to have a radio station of your own?"

I told him that, naturally, I'd love to have one of my own. But in my wildest dreams I knew I could never own one. I just could not afford to buy a radio station..

He said, "Find one and we'll buy it."

So I started shopping around. I shopped in North Carolina and other places, trying to find a small-market station. The owner of station WCON in Cornelia, Mr. Jack Bradley, found out that I was "in the market" and called me into his office one day. "Are you serious about this?" he asked.

I told him that I was.

So he said, "You know, I built a station in Sandersville, Georgia, and I'll sell it to you."

I had never been to Sandersville, Georgia, in my life, but I said I would go look at it. So I did. It was a "right nice" little radio station, WSNT. And so my uncle bought it; he wrote them a check for it.

But he didn't give the station to me. I had to pay him back for it. So every time I made him a payment, he considered half of it already to be his, and he would allow only the other half to go toward paying the debt. So, in truth, I was paying a generous return. But that's how it is when you have nothing. As the saying goes, "Beggars can't be choosers."

But it was not the bed of roses I had imagined. I had an extremely hard struggle and some very trying times in the beginning. The people there were wonderful. I enjoyed the community; it was great. But the thing that was difficult was the payment I needed to make to my uncle. One thing that helped was that I brought down an announcer who had worked with WCON when it first started. He came in and joined me, and through his support, help, and encouragement, I kept holding on. But my payments were hard to make. I was down: sometimes I couldn't pay myself anything. If I could buy my meals, I felt good.

But I had an interesting little lesson while I was going through those trying times. I think any time you go through trying times, you can take that experience and build from it and use it as an academic experience to build whatever you envision that you want to build from it.

The lesson I learned involved two big grocery stores there. One of the grocery stores, which was independently owned, was my best advertiser. The other grocery store was a very small advertiser, but was part of a big chain. The independent store, which was my best advertiser, advertised enough for me to make my payments. Without that store I don't know if I could have made those payments. That store was very critical to me.

One day the owner of that store told me that for him to continue to advertise with me, I would have to agree to discontinue accepting ads from the competitor grocery store after he gave me his ad. That way, his competitor could not cut prices, based on his ad.

I told him, "I can't do that. That is morally wrong. That's one of the advantages of radio: you can cut your price every fifteen minutes if you so desire. Once it's printed in the newspaper, it's printed, and that's all you can do for the whole week, but you have versatility with radio."

He said, "Well, it's up to you. Those are my terms." He made
it clear that if I didn't agree to his terms, he would discontinue all
his advertising with me.

Now, you talk about someone who was under unbelievable
stress: I was. I faced the most horrible thing that could happen to
a man at that time, and that is that I wouldn't be able to succeed.
I had to choose between what I thought was morally right on the
one hand and, on the other, what I needed to do, it seemed, to be
successful. And I chose to do what I thought was morally right.

Now, I must say I'm convinced that the guy who was pushing
me to ban his competitor was not really trying to hurt me. I
never took it that way, and I'm sure he had what he thought were
legitimate reasons for doing what he did. I'm not throwing him
under the bus. But he canceled his advertising, every bit of it.

I thought, "What am I going to do?"

But one day shortly thereafter I went over to the other grocery
store to pick up their ad, which was nothing compared to what
the other store had been running. I'm sure I looked like warmed-
over death as I walked in, causing the manager to ask, "John,
what in the world is wrong with you? You look like you've lost
your best friends."

I said, "Well, I admit I have a problem that I would never had
imagined I would be confronted with, and I don't know where
my future lies."

He wanted me to explain to him what I meant, so I just
honestly explained the situation to him. And he said, "Come
up here to my office a minute; I want to make a phone call." We
went to his office, and he called the headquarters of his company
and explained to them what had happened.

He listened for a while, and then he turned around and said,
"John, how much advertising were they doing with you?" And I
told him.

He talked with his company's headquarters for several more
minutes; then he hung up and said to me, "I tell you what we're
going to do, John. We're going to take *all* the advertising. We're

going to buy as much advertising as they were doing; plus we're going to do so much more. We're going to give away a five-dollar bill every hour on the hour to the lucky shopper who has got the right numbered buggy, and we'll see if we can't change things for you."

I couldn't believe it. His store started running a lot of ads right away, and by the next weekend the other guy's parking lot was just about empty. The next week, it was the same way. The next week I got a phone call from the guy who owned the independent store. He wanted me to come back and see him, so I did.

He said, "John, you're winning. If you'll pull off, we'll go back to advertising like we were before."

I said, "I can't. I'm not the one that's doing it. I mean, I'm just accepting advertising and running it. I can't tell a grocery store that I won't accept its advertising."

To make a long story short, he opted to begin advertising with us again. But the other store continued to do a lot of advertising, too, for quite some time afterwards, and the manager of that store literally saved me and my business.

Everything turned out fine, and I really think it's because I acted based on my conviction that if you do what is morally right, you'll ultimately win out. Maybe you won't win immediately, but you will ultimately win out. And if nothing else, your conscience will be clean.

We began to succeed reasonably well—never really, really well—but we could make our payments. Later, another nice station in Washington, Georgia, came up for sale, and I bought that station. Well, I should say that Uncle Webster again backed me, and we bought it.

I bought that station with the idea that I would utilize the guy who was my newsman at the Sandersville station as the general manager of the new station. His name was Frank Roughton. He was a good friend, a very bright, capable guy. Unfortunately, I had said nothing to him about it. I had just assumed that he would be thrilled to death when I called him in and told him what I wanted him to do. But when I called Frank in and told him that I wanted him to be the manager of the new station, he said, "John, I don't think I can do it."

I said, "What! You mean you're not going to take the management of this new station?"

"I'll let you know tomorrow," he said.

I said, "You've got to be crazy, man. You just recently got married. You bought a new Buick station wagon. You're just starting out here, and this is a great opportunity for you."

He again told me that he would let me know tomorrow.

The next day he came in and I said, "Well, Frank, what's your decision?"

He said, "My decision is that I'm quitting."

I said, "You've got to be kidding. You just bought the new car. You've got a new wife. What in the world has come over you?"

He said, "I'm going into the ministry. I feel like the Lord's calling me to be a preacher." And he told me that he was going to start out doing the Sermon on the Mount.

Well, Frank Roughton went on to become a nationally known evangelist under the name Frank Roughton Harvey. He lived in Kentucky and was still a dear friend at the time of his death. He put on passion plays, dramatizing the life of Christ and other Biblical characters, all over the country. On one occasion, he did so at the old Atlanta Stadium—with Dr. Border Holmes, I believe was his name—where he played the part of Christ or one of the major roles, and they literally filled that stadium.

I have a lot of respect for what Frank Roughton did. I'm not a minister, but I've always been guided by my faith. For example, since the day I started out in broadcasting, I have never accepted beer, liquor, or wine advertising. I've been in this business since the 1950s, and I have never accepted a dime for advertising from that sector. Never. Now, that doesn't mean the station hasn't ever advertised wine or beer or other kinds of alcohol, because I can't control what comes over the networks. But I've never accepted such advertising locally.

Also, ever since I've been in the business, I have never broadcast a day that I didn't do some programming for Christ. I've never backed away from that: I do it every single day. When we expanded to our big 50-thousand watt FM station, I continued to do that programming. I do it to this day. And until the day I leave the industry, I will continue to do so. It's what I want to do, and I think that the Lord has blessed me greatly because I have been faithful to him. I really do.

*****

But the greatest thing that ever happened to me occurred in the late 1950s when I was living in Sandersville: Bobbie, who became my wife, finally decided to marry me. A friend of ours first introduced us when I was managing the theater. I was overwhelmed with her just on a social date, a double date with some friends. I asked her if she would go out with me again, and she said okay. She had a car, but all I had was my family's old truck, so I would go to her house in that old truck, and then we'd go out in her car. I think she was a little embarrassed riding around in an old big truck. But the uniqueness of it all is the fact that I proposed to her right off the bat on our second date, which was really our first date in a way.

For me, it was love at first sight. I thought, "Hey, this is the one." But it wasn't that way for her. She never would say no, but she would always say that she had to be sure. We went on to date for about four years. Finally, one day she said, "Okay, I guess it's time."

I was already in Sandersville when she agreed to marry me, and she was teaching school in Cornelia. She had finished college and was teaching at age eighteen, I believe it was. She was pretty amazing. Needless to say, she has been my greatest blessing through the years.

We married, and from that day on we were partners, in business and in life.

6. WCON, Cornelia

In the late 1950s, I owned two radio stations – one in Sandersville, Georgia, and one in Washington, Georgia. However, my dream was to own my hometown station: WCON in Cornelia. One weekend I was in Cornelia visiting, and late Saturday afternoon I stopped by WCON to say hello to the station's owner, Jack Bradley.

"How would you like to buy this station?" he asked.

"I'd love that," I said. "Give me a little while to think about it."

A little later that evening I called him back and told him I would take it. I did not know how I was going to pay for it; I was already in debt with my other two stations. But I felt in my heart that I could sell them.

I called up a friend, Johnny Bailes, who lived in Swainsboro, Georgia. He managed station WJAT in Swainsboro and was a big name in country music; he used to sing with the Bailes Brothers. I told him that I was thinking about selling the radio stations in Sandersville and Washington, and I asked him if he was interested in them. He said that he was and that he would come visit me so that we could talk about it. I explained to him that I was going to buy my hometown station in Cornelia

A few days later, a group of three guys arrived to see me: Johnny Bailes; Webb Pierce, the country music singer; and Jim Denny, the music and record publisher. I was somewhat awed that Webb Pierce was there: he was a big-time country music singer at that time.

They ended up looking at both stations. They decided they didn't want the Washington station, but they did want to buy the Sandersville station. So I priced it to them. Naturally, if you're smart, you're going to price something higher than what you think you can get. You can always come down in price, but you can't go up. So I priced it a bit high, and they said okay. They still got a good deal on it, but it was a *very* good deal for me. That sale provided me with the money I needed to buy WCON in 1961. Eventually, I sold the Washington station to a businessman from Charlotte, North Carolina.

To buy WCON, I also had to buy a small station, which was in Buford, Georgia. WCON was the only station I wanted to own, so I practically gave away the Buford station. That's the number one dumbest mistake I've ever made in my life. I hate to think what that station is worth today.

However, selling that station allowed me to concentrate on just one station. I could always do pretty well with a radio station that I personally managed. Whenever I delegated a station to other people, it never was as successful as I thought it should be. At one point I really wanted to expand into owning a chain of radio stations. But as I progressed, I found out that if I personally managed a station and looked after it, I could do fairly well. So I forgot about owning multiple stations and decided to concentrate on just one. And I'm glad I did.

In the early 1960s, WCON was an AM station only. I believed that FM had a future, so I applied for an FM license and got it. We then put an FM station on the air and started programming good music, easy-listening music. In the beginning, there weren't many people listening to FM radio. Sometimes our automation system would break down, leaving us without any audio going out for an hour or two, and we would never get a phone call about it. Eventually, however, FM began to pick up, and that's how we are able to have the WCON-FM that we have today, a powerful one-hundred-thousand-watt station.

John in overalls, 1937.

School photo, circa 1949.

High-school football, 1953.

School photo, circa 1953.

In the military, 1954.

John at WSNT, 1957.

John in a suit and tie, 1957.

Bobbie and John's wedding day, with family, 1958.

John at WSNT, 1959.

7. Running for Public Office

Before I got involved in politics, it never occurred to me that I would some day run for public office. It never crossed my mind.

I had been active in civic organizations since the early 1960s. I held office in several of them. I got involved in Jaycees and became president. I was president of the Chamber of Commerce three times. One year while I was president, we were successful in locating the Regal textile plant here, which was a 20-million dollar plant. That was a huge accomplishment in those days. Also, while president, I felt that we needed to build the infrastructure in the community so that we could attract more industry. Natural gas was one of the things I felt was critical to the community, so that became one major focus. We also began implementing plans for an airport. Dean Swanson is the guy who took the bull by the horns on that project, and the airport was recently named in his honor. Before it was built, he and I got out there and walked the land, measuring the fields for it

I want to emphasize that none of my successes were the result of my efforts alone; they were always accomplished through teamwork. In my judgment, the key to succeeding is putting together the right team to do the job. And I was fortunate to have so many good partners available in Cornelia.

At any rate, I just seemed to evolve into holding office. At a certain point I began to get *some* encouragement to run for public office, but not a whole lot of encouragement. I used to think I had a lot of encouragement, but I think human beings have a tendency to exaggerate such things because we want to think that a lot of people believe in us.

I began to feel some motivation to run for public office, but it was not for the ego boost. That never was part of my motivation. My motivation to be in public life was the fact that it could put me in position to be more effective in doing things for the people in my community. It would open up doors that could help us. Having a local business was part of my motivation, simply because if the community grew, my business would also grow. If the community grew, our people would prosper as well. Eventually I decided that I wanted to run for public office.

In 1970, I decided to run for the Georgia House of Representatives. I ran against former Commissioner of Agriculture, Tommy Irvin, who was the incumbent representative at that time. In the election, he beat the socks off of me, beat me about three to one. Needless to say, it was embarrassing.

I knew, I just *knew*, that the good Lord had wanted me to run. I've heard people say that they're running for office, and they've prayed about it, and the Lord wants them to run. I have learned that it's fine to pray about it, if you want to do that, but we must remember that what we think the Lord wants may not coincide with what He actually wants. It is easy for us to mislead ourselves.

Anyway, Tommy and I were friends and remained friends until his death. I had a couple of people who got behind me and encouraged me to run in that first election, but I did not realize at the time that they were actually mad at Tommy. They made me think I could do something, but I wasn't angry with Tommy when I ran against him; I just thought I could win. Finding out that some of those who encouraged me to run against him weren't really for me in the first place was a lesson that I learned the hard way.

Later, Tommy moved on to greener pastures and bigger and better things, so I decided that I would run for the House of Representatives again in 1972. I ran against a great fellow; neither of us was an incumbent, but he was a much older, more established businessperson in the community. I lost again, although this time I lost by fewer than thirty votes.

At this point I was saying to myself, "You know, maybe the Lord really doesn't want me to be in politics." I had serious doubts about ever running for public office again.

However, I was learning an important lesson: how to read politics. I don't know that you can ever really know how to read, for lack of a better expression, "the tea leaves of politics." But one thing that I had to learn was the fact that when you're in the political arena, you have to recognize that, no matter how idealistic you are, you are of no value unless you can get elected and remain elected. Consequently, you have to learn how to balance your idealism with practical realism.

This was a lesson that I had to learn. When I first started out, I would go out and talk to people, and they would tell me their views on the issues. If I disagreed with them, I would immediately tell them, "Why, I don't agree with that at all. I would never support a position like that."

Well, by doing that, I was losing votes both left and right. I was telling the truth, but I found out that in politics, sometimes it is better to say nothing. If you are out there politicking, give people an opportunity to express their views, but unless they say something that's just overwhelmingly outrageous, either keep your views to yourself, or simply say to them, "Well, that certainly is an interesting perspective, one to think about." When I didn't argue with people, I didn't make them mad, and they knew that I was at least willing to listen to them. Consequently, I had a chance of gaining their votes.

Another lesson I learned is that you have to be honest with yourself. You absolutely must! Also, you find out that when people tell you they'll support you, at least fifty percent of them won't. That happened to me again and again.

Another good lesson I learned is about campaign contributions. Originally, I would tell people that I didn't want any contributions from them, that I wasn't going to be beholden to anybody. That's stupid, as I learned the hard way. You want to get every contribution you can get, if it's legitimate and within the framework of your convictions.

Those are the kinds of lessons I was learning, but by this time I really didn't know if I would ever run for public office again. I had about decided that I had been reading the Lord's will for me incorrectly.

Nevertheless, I did still have a deep, inner feeling that I would like to be a servant leader for the cause of humankind. That was a deep-seated feeling of mine. Also, I had reached a point where I wanted to see if I could win a race. I wanted to prove that I could win at least one race.

I decided that I would run for the Georgia Senate in the 1974 election. A friend who was in the senate at the time was going to run for Lieutenant Governor, and I talked to him about my running for the senate. He later changed his mind and ran again for the senate, but by that time I had already made a commitment to people that I would run for the senate.

I had been going around and talking to people and asking them, "Would you help me? Can you make me a contribution?"

All of a sudden, I saw that people were willing to make generous contributions to my campaign. But they would also say to me, "If I make a commitment to you, will you make a commitment to me?" The only commitment they wanted from me was this: "Will you commit to run?" I gave them my word that I would.

When my friend decided not to run for lieutenant governor but to run for the senate again, that really bothered me. I never intended to run against him. On the other hand, I had made a commitment to run. I felt morally obligated to keep my commitment, so I ran. I didn't win the first go around, but I did end up in a runoff with the incumbent; another candidate had entered the race and caused a runoff. Finally, in the runoff, I won. Needless to say, that was an interesting day in my life.

I never will forget the first phone call I got the morning after that election. Governor Jimmy Carter was calling to congratulate me.

8. Early Days in the Georgia Senate

When I went to the senate, some interesting things happened to me because I was so green and immature. I didn't think I was at the time, but looking back, I realize I was. I started off wanting to ask a lot of questions, and I wanted to get a lot of attention. I soon found out, however, that that approach wasn't getting me anywhere.

I began to search my own life. What do I want out of this? Why am I here? I realized that I was in the senate to serve people. Being a senator is a great honor. It's a real honor to be elected by the people to represent them. But being in the senate, as far as the legislative process is concerned, was never that thrilling of an experience for me.

The part that I enjoyed the most was being of service to people. As a senator, I was in a position to help people, to do things for them, to intercede on their behalf. One of the greatest experiences I ever had while in office is a good example of this. I hadn't been in office long when a single mother and her son came to see me. The woman wept as she tried to talk to me. She said that her son had to have back surgery or he would die. She asked me, "Can you help me somehow? Can you open a door for me and let him get that surgery?"

I immediately went to work. I called a friend who had a friend connected with Egleston Hospital. Within three days, the boy was in Egleston. He had the surgery, and it was successful. A few years later I was at a service station, putting gas in my car, when a fine-looking young man walked up to me and said, "Senator Foster?"

"Yes," I said.

"Do you recognize me?" he asked.

I looked at him and said, "No. I'm sorry; I don't."

He then reminded me of the morning that a mother and her son had come to see me, and he said, "I'm that boy."

I have never had anything touch me so. I was thrilled to see him, and I asked him how his mother was doing.

"Fine," he said. Then immediately he added, "She's in heaven."

To me, being able to help people is what life is all about. As a senator, I had so many opportunities to be of service to people. Even to this day, I help people whenever I can. People still call me, asking if I can help them. I very much enjoyed that aspect of being a legislator.

But there were aspects I didn't enjoy. Basically, legislative bodies are simply reactionary bodies. For instance, this is something that I wrote years ago when I was president of the Piedmont College Alumni Association:

Crisis breeds action, which during your lifetime has often been passionate but irrational. But crisis also generates impatience toward lifestyle institutions which were not born in the atmosphere of crisis. This combination of impulsive action and its inherent impatience . . . furnishes the theme songs for protest marches.

In other words, we, as legislators, were constantly reacting to crises. That remains true today.

9. Speech Writing

As a senator, I wrote and delivered probably 500 speeches, but I was fortunate to find a speechwriter, Richard M. Austin, who worked with me and provided invaluable help. He worked for the Georgia Department of Corrections. He was a maverick sort of guy, and he was a compassionate human being. And he was brilliant.

Our connection began shortly after I was elected, I realized that I needed help writing speeches, so I began seeking out someone who could help me. If I had one strong suit, it was the ability to recognize what I didn't know or couldn't do.

I was talking to a friend at church one day, and I told him that I needed somebody to help me with my speeches, but I didn't have any money. He told me to go see Dick Austin. I'd never met Dick before, but I went to his house to talk to him. He was wearing a cowboy hat and cowboy boots; he was a sight to behold. I asked him whether he could write speeches.

"Yes, I can," he said. "As a matter of fact, I'm good at it."

I didn't know what to think. I said, "Oh, you're good at it, huh?"

He said, "Yes, I'm good at it." That's the way he was.

I told Dick that I'd been invited to speak at the University of Georgia: this was one of the very first speaking opportunities I had as a newly elected senator. "I've been invited to speak down there to the gerontology society," I said, "but I'm not sure I know what *gerontology* means exactly."

He said, "*I* know."

I asked, "What can you say to a group of folks like that?"

"I know a lot of things we can say," he said.

He agreed to help me. The next day I went back to his house, and he handed me a speech he had written for me and had me read it back to him.

"You can't read the way I write," he said. "I've got to rework this to make it fit the way you speak." He rewrote the speech and had me read it to him again.

"I need to simplify it," he said, "because your speaking style is basically a simple one."

He rewrote the speech again, and this time the words began to flow. I could see that this guy was a genius at putting words together.

He went on to give me some advice. He told me that I should read the speech many, many times, but that I shouldn't try to memorize it. He said I should learn it well enough that I wouldn't have to read it word for word to the audience. He said I should know exactly what I wanted to say so that I could say it the way I wanted it to be said. He explained that I didn't want to have my words read back to me the next day and find out that I had made some careless error of statement. I always thought that was pretty good advice.

When the time came, I went down to the University of Georgia and gave that speech. I was scared to death; the experience reminded me of my 4-H presentation. I was petrified, but I struggled through it. I thought I did a miserable job; I thought I had failed. Afterwards, however, about a dozen people came up to me and asked me for copies of that speech. I thought, "Holy cow! They want copies of my speech!" That was the first experience I had of people requesting copies of my speeches. I knew right then that Dick Austin was meant to be a partner in writing the speeches that I would deliver as a senator.

Dick wrote that first speech for me, but we collaborated on the rest of them. We would sit and talk, and he would take notes. Afterwards, it didn't take him long to bring me a finished speech. We were quite a team.

I used to say to him, "Dick, I feel so inadequate in expressing to you my appreciation and awe for all you do for me."

He would say, "Let me tell you something. I feel good about what I'm doing with you because, through you, I'm getting to help achieve some things that I'd like to see achieved in life."

He never would try to influence me to think like him or to take certain positions. If I asked him his opinion about something, he would tell me, but he would always tell me that the final decision was mine. "You're the senator," he would say. "You're the guy who has to make the decision."

Dick ended up working with me for many years. When he died, I lost a good friend. I owe a lot to him.

*****

One of the requirements that I always had for the people I worked with was that they be candidly honest with me. Also, I always tried to surround myself with people that I felt really knew what they were doing. If they couldn't do a better job than I could do, I didn't want them around.

During my tenure as senator, I was fortunate to have a number of outstanding people who worked with me and whose help was absolutely invaluable. I hesitate to name them because I know I would leave somebody out. I hope that they know who they are and that they have my gratitude.

I was also fortunate to have some very special friends, who helped me in so many ways.

To everyone who helped me, I will always be grateful.

10. President Carter

During Jimmy Carter's term as president, I introduced a resolution for the Georgia Senate to honor President Carter. Because I introduced it, Governor Zell Miller appointed me to chair the committee formed to handle the matter.

We wanted to commission a portrait of the president and hang it in the senate. We called President Carter and asked him if he would agree to sit for a painting. We told him that we would pay for it privately, without using any public funds, and we asked him if he would consider coming to Atlanta for the unveiling ceremony. He agreed to everything. He picked the artist he wanted to do the painting, and we paid the artist through private contributions.

The unveiling turned out to be one of the most exciting opportunities ever handed to me: President Carter asked me to be the one to unveil the portrait. That is an honor and an experience that I will never forget.

The arrangements and preparations for the president's visit to Atlanta were themselves pretty amazing. The FBI and the Secret Service came days in advance to check out everyone and everything. They checked me out from stem to stern before giving me security clearance. They rented an entire upper floor of the Peachtree Plaza Hotel, where they installed what seemed like tons of radio gear. They even had wireless phones, which weren't common at all back then. Their communication system ensured that the president was never more than a few feet away from a direct phone line to the White House.

Thanks to my security clearance, I got to see how the president moves around. Just to move the president of the United States from one point to another requires much planning and the working out of many details.

On the morning of the unveiling, I received a copy of the president's agenda, and I couldn't believe how thick that document was. It said the president would be awakened at this hour, and he would have breakfast at that hour. It specified which people would see him off in Washington. It listed who would be at Dobbins Air Force Base in Marietta to greet him at the specified time. It even explained where they would be standing. It contained an incredible level of detail.

*****

I have fond memories of my visits and talks with President Carter. He routinely invited me over to the Carter Center. Every year, he had a get-together with a lot of folks, maybe a hundred or so. Afterwards there would be a discussion session, and I enjoyed those sessions tremendously.

He and I had a lot of private conversations, too. Getting my Secret Service clearance made things a lot easier because then, when I visited the White House, I could go right in. The Secret Service would verify my clearance, then tell me to go ahead.

I got to tour the White House many times. I never saw the upstairs dining room or living quarters, but I didn't desire to do so. That area was private and part of the president's personal life. However, I got to tour the president's office and the staff offices. I got to walk in the rose garden and to eat in the downstairs private dining facility. It was exciting for me, someone who began life on a farm in Cornelia, Georgia, finding myself a guest of the president of the United States, who also came from a farm in Georgia. Even now, it seems to me to be proof that the American dream can become reality.

*****

President Carter has always been very good to me. When he was governor, he supported me and came up to my district to campaign on my behalf. I have always remembered that, and I appreciate it to this day. When he decided to run for president in the 1976 election, I let him know that if he didn't get but two votes, they would be his and mine.

During his 1976 campaign, I became part of his "Peanut Brigade," a group of supporters who traveled the country to campaign for him. I was sent to Kentucky. I went there by myself and traveled around, campaigning for him and helping to coordinate his campaign in particular areas.

One day, on my way to Elizabethtown, Kentucky, I was listening to a local radio station. I noticed that they were running a bunch of spots for Carter's opponent, Gerald Ford, but none for Jimmy Carter. So I went to that station: being in broadcasting, I knew how the system worked. I walked in, and there was nobody there but one announcer. I asked him if he had any spots for Jimmy Carter, and he said no.

"Well," I said, "I want to buy some."

"I don't have time to record them right now," he said.

I said, "I'll tell you what I'll do. If you give me access to a typewriter, I'll write the commercial, and then I'll record it. And I'll pay for it in cash right now."

He said okay, so I wrote and recorded some commercials. After the election, I learned that President Carter won in that area. I don't know whether my commercials had any effect, but getting them on the air was a lot of fun.

Actually, the whole campaign was a lot of fun. However, when you are out there representing a candidate who is running to be President of the United States, you have to realize that anything you say or do can be reflected upon him. You really have to weigh what you say and how you act. It's pretty serious business.

11. Piedmont College

Besides politics and my church, another point of pride for me, and one of the most exciting of all I've ever been involved in, that I'm just so thrilled to be a part of, is Piedmont College. Not only did I graduate from Piedmont College; I never will forget when the president of the college said to me, "John, some day I want you to be on our board of trustees." I thought, "*Me* be on the board of trustees? Trustees are the big donors; I can't afford to be a big donor." That's what I thought, anyway.

Now, my uncle was already on the board of trustees. My uncle, Dr. Claude Purcell (my mother's brother), was the state superintendent of schools. He was also the one who got me to choose education as my focus when I went into the senate. He not only was on the board of trustees of Piedmont College, he was chairman of that board for many years. So when the president mentioned to me about coming on the board, I told him I didn't want to do so while my uncle was still serving because we had such different views of how a college should function. I didn't want to clash with my uncle, so I didn't accept the offer.

Later, after my uncle passed away, I was again invited to come on the board of trustees, and this time I did. We had 250 to 300 students back then, and the board was very controversial. I hated every minute of it. Jim Walters was no longer president, but he had handpicked his successor. The board at this time was really a body made up of dictators; the students were of secondary concern to them. Finally, however, a change was made. Another person came in on a temporary basis. And then I got elected chairman of the board of trustees. I hadn't sought that position, but they wanted me to do it, so I said okay.

The man who was president of the college called me in one day and told me that he was retiring. I thought, "Man, you have got to be out of your head. You're retiring, leaving me saddled with this college?" But I found out that I actually was to be the one who was in charge. I was to be the one who called the shots on how the next president would be picked. This was clearly stated in the bylaws.

Prior to this, the chairman had always picked his personal favorite. We had two or three people on our board who were very strong people, and, knowing the precedent, they had already started picking the president that they wanted.

But I said, "Wait a minute. I'm chairman of the board, and we're going to use a new process this year." So I appointed a search committee, made up of faculty, administration, students, trustees, and alumni. And I gave them directions. I appointed a chairman of the search committee, who had never been involved much with the board, because I perceived that unless I intervened, the two or three dominant trustees—they were the dictators—wouldn't let anybody else be involved.

When I issued these instructions, one particular trustee went ballistic. He was absolutely beside himself that I would do such a thing. I didn't ask him beforehand. I didn't even invite him to be on the committee. I told him, "No, I don't want you on the committee. If I had wanted you on it, I would have put you on it."

I put other people on the committee; my plan was that we were going to broaden our perspective. I wanted every board member to feel included in the process. However, this angry trustee wrote a scathing letter about me to every one of the trustees, saying what a dictator I had become. In fact, *he* was the dictator, or was at least trying to be. But to make a long story short, no one agreed with him. He never got one letter of support. I, however, got several letters that said I was doing exactly the right thing.

So we went through that selection process, and I had nothing to do with selecting the three candidates who would be recommended to the board. I stayed completely out of it. The committee recommended three people to review, and the Board of Trustees Executive Committee and I interviewed the three prospects privately. One of them happened to be a personal friend of mine. I had no idea that he had applied. He didn't need to talk to me; he was a chancellor of the university system of Mississippi, and he used to be a vice chairman of the University of Georgia. But he was ready to slow down and wanted to be president of a small college. Also, he was familiar with this college. But I still did not try to use any influence at all. I was hoping he would be the one who would be picked. But I didn't intervene: I wanted us to follow the process and pick the best candidate. As it turned out, the board unanimously selected the candidate that I wanted, Dr. Ray Cleere. Dr. Cleere was one of the most exciting, visionary leaders I've ever been around.

At that time, Piedmont College had an enrollment of over two-thousand students. During my time as chairman of the board, we spent over thirty-million dollars rebuilding the campus. We had a fifty-million-dollar endowment. In the fall of 2005, we awarded a contract for a new ten-million dollar fine-arts center. As I good-humoredly told some folks one day, "By golly, I take credit for this whole damn thing because I'm the guy who put the committee together that recommended this president."

Piedmont is such a wonderful campus now. It has new libraries, and we don't owe much money, either. Also, we don't accept federal monies. The only way we make any money that's federally related is through the Pell Grant programs for the students. We will not take a federal grant. We have done it on our own, and we have done it quite well. We have a chapel with a million-dollar organ in it. We have a gym that is second to none. We have a baseball field that cost over a million dollars. We own all of Johnny Mize's baseball memorabilia and have a Johnny Mize museum.

I am proud of my affiliation with Piedmont College. It was a labor of love. But it all boils down to leadership and to Ray

Cleere. He was a nationally recognized leader before he ever came here, and he was such a visionary that he received complete and total support from the board of trustees. How he could see so far down the road the way he did amazed me.

For example, Piedmont now has a campus in Athens, Georgia. When Ray told me that they were going to propose to the board that we open a campus in Athens, Georgia, I said, "You must have lost your mind. The University of Georgia is in Athens."

"No," he said, "the University of Georgia supports us."

I said, "They support us?"

He said, "Yes. Everybody can't go to the university, and Athens doesn't have a college."

As always, he was right.

You cannot overstate the value of an education. As I used to say so often, "Education is the ultimate emancipator of a society. If you want to see your country go down the tubes, just let it continue to be uneducated." To see the success of Piedmont College is one of the things that fills me with pride and joy.

John with family, 1974.

Senator John Foster standing in front of the Georgia State Capitol, 1978.

Senator Foster unveiling a portrait of President Jimmy Carter at the
Georgia State Capitol, 1984.

John with family, 1985.

Receiving an Honorary Doctorate from Piedmont College, 1990.

Induction into the Georgia Association of Broadcasters Hall of Fame, 2015.

The Foster family, 2019.

12. Reflections on the Senate

I was first elected to the Georgia Senate in 1974. I took office in January 1975 and served through 1992. That was a wonderful experience for me, and I am deeply honored to have held that office.

Serving in the senate, however, did sometimes bring its share of frustrations. For example, in 1976, when I was still fairly new in the senate, I introduced a resolution establishing a water-study committee to deal with Georgia's future water problems. That same year, we held hearings on that issue all over the state. We kept bringing what we were learning to the attention of the political leadership. We told them about the water crisis that our state would face in the future. We told them that by the year 2000 we were going to be facing major water problems, problems that had already begun to occur. However, we couldn't get enough people to listen, and those problems still have not been adequately dealt with today. That was especially frustrating.

Too often, legislators don't look beyond the next election. We need to look ahead to the future, to assess how our actions or inactions will affect our state and our citizens twenty-five years from now. Every time we make a move, we should ask ourselves how it will affect our people not just today, but also tomorrow. Similarly, we should ask ourselves whether something is enhancing the pockets of a certain group or industry or is actually something good for the entire state and its communities. We could save untold millions of dollars. But far more importantly, we could make our state a better place for our children and for future generations.

I learned early during my tenure that standing up for what you believe can make you extremely unpopular with those who disagree with you. For example, I once took a strong stand that labeling well water as "spring water" should not be allowed. To allow such labeling would be dishonest, I believed, because well water is *not* spring water. Predictably, one fellow who had a strong financial interest in that issue became very angry with me over my stand.

The teachers unions are another example. I didn't believe in teachers unions, and as a matter of fact I still don't. Whenever a teachers union sent me a contribution, I always returned it. Consequently, the teachers unions didn't like me. I never will forget the two different occasions when they wrote letters to all their members, telling them that I never voted for pay raises for teachers. Their statement was a bold-faced lie, yet some of the teachers believed it.

I had to take positions; that's part of the job. Being the chairman of a committee, I had to take positions that were good for the entire state of Georgia, not just my district. Consequently, some of my counties were hurt sometimes. But I had to look out for the whole state. When you're in a leadership position, such as the chair of a committee, and if you're honoring your responsibility, you have to represent every citizen of the state. I hoped that my constituents would recognize that, but too often they did not.

Seeing fellow legislators not honor their responsibility was always a big disappointment. I've seen legislators on such ego trips that they seemed to think only of themselves. Some became very powerful and did things they should not have done. One time a legislator told me that he wouldn't serve on certain committees because he couldn't make any money off of them. Now, I don't mean to impugn the legislative body; it's a wonderful body and a wonderful process. There were some great legislators there during my terms in office, and there are some great legislators there today. Unfortunately, it seems there will always be a few bad apples.

The reason I bring up these negative experiences from my public life is that I want to paint an accurate and realistic picture. I don't want to gloss over the negative aspects and present a falsely rosy account. However, I certainly don't mean to suggest that my experience as a senator was negative; it was far from it. I am honored to have served, and I feel very privileged to have been in a position that enabled me to help people and to help bring about needed change.

Sometimes, even a negative experience would ultimately bring about a positive one. Once I got into a very heated confrontation with some constituents over an issue regarding someone who wanted a piece of legislation introduced locally. Another group didn't want to introduce the legislation locally, and the pressure became so great on us that it was almost unbearable. I had given the group that didn't want the legislation introduced my word that I wouldn't introduce it. However, that made no difference to the other group; they kept applying the pressure.

Finally I told them, "Look, I'm not going to do it. I gave my word, and consequently, I'm not going to do it. Now, there will be an election next year, and that will be your opportunity to judge me, but I must do what I said I would do. So don't bother me about this anymore."

Later that summer, on a Sunday afternoon, I got a phone call from the leader of that group.

He said, "John, I have learned some things since we last talked about this issue, and you are absolutely right." Then he added, "As long as you are running, I will always vote for you."

I thought that it took a heck of a lot of guts for that person to call and tell me that. And it brought home to me that people appreciate their public servants being straightforward with them.

I had a similar experience in Union County, when I was a young elected official and the Equal Rights Amendment was a hotly debated issue. A majority of my constituents were in favor of the amendment, and that is, in fact, why I supported it. However, another reason I made a commitment to support it is that I thought it was the right thing to do. I thought it was one of those principles that really deserved our support because I never believed that God thought more of me than He did my wife. I believed that He loved us both equally.

When I was first elected, I started holding public hearings before every session. I went around to all eight counties in my district, and held a public hearing in each one. I did that every year that I was in public office. I published announcements of the hearings in the local newspapers, and I also published a questionnaire. The last question was always this:: "Are you satisfied with the way I represent you? Yes or no, and if no, what may I do to improve?" I would also hand out copies of the questionnaire at the hearings.

One year, I didn't have a question about the Equal Rights Amendment on the questionnaire because I already knew that I was going to vote for it. I didn't see any point in discussing it. Of course, I was willing to discuss it if somebody so desired, but I didn't need further input to help me make up my mind.

Anyway, at the public hearing in Union County, the audience included a hundred people from a particular church. As I was discussing my questionnaire, one of them got up and said, "We want to talk with you about the Equal Rights Amendment."

I stood up and walked out into the middle of them, and I said, "I'm willing to talk about it. What do you want to say?"

The person said, "We're all against it."

"I surmised that," I said.

Someone then asked whether I wanted to see a show of hands.

"No, I don't," I said, "because I know you are against it. But I'm not changing my mind. And I'm going to tell you why I'm not changing my mind: I am for it for the very same reason that you are against it."

The people looked confused.

"You believe that opposing it is the Christian thing to do," I said, "but I believe firmly in my heart that for me to support it is the Christian thing to do. I'm convinced that God made us all equal, and I'm going to vote for it. I'm telling you right here and now that I'm going to vote for it when it comes before the senate."

You could have heard a pin drop.

Well, everyone had a copy of the questionnaire, and they filled them out while we were discussing other issues. After the hearing, I was so anxious to find out how they answered the question about whether they were satisfied with me that I stopped along the way. I pulled off to the side of the road and read through all of those questionnaires. Of all the questionnaires that were filled out, there were only three that said the person was unhappy with me. That experience taught me a "whale" of a lesson, and that is, some of the public will always disagree with you. However, if you can give them a sincere, convincing argument for why you're taking a certain position on something, they will respect you. Those kinds of experiences, I believe, made me a better legislator through the years.

Another rewarding aspect of my public service career was my opportunity to participate in national organizations. For example, I represented the senate nationally on the Southern Regional Education Board, and I chaired the education committee for that organization. Such opportunities are valuable because they expose you to ideas from other states, and sometimes they enable you to meet people who are well known. For instance, one day at White Sulfur Springs, West Virginia, when Bill Clinton was governor of Arkansas, I spoke on the same platform with Hillary Clinton.

Overall, I am deeply honored to have served nine terms in the Georgia Senate, and I am proud of what I was able to accomplish. I introduced a variety of legislation, For example, I introduced the legislation that brought the Olympics to Georgia in 1996. Education, however, was always my primary interest. I replaced Hugh Carter on the education committee following his retirement, and I served in that capacity until I left the senate.

I also made many good friends during my years in the senate. Zell Miller lived in my district. He was always very good to me, and we were good friends until his passing. President Carter has always been good to me. Sam Nunn and Herman Talmadge were also good to me.

Lester Maddox, governor of Georgia from 1967 to 1971, was an interesting friend. He was an unusual character in many ways, but he was a very compassionate human being. I hadn't gotten involved in politics when he was governor, but in his later years, when he was ill, he took a liking to me for some reason or another, and he would call me every so often. In fact, the last time I talked to him, he was bedridden and didn't live too long after that. He told me that he was too ill to write to me anymore, that he could only talk on the telephone. So I would call him and listen to how he was doing.

I cannot list all of the friends that I met during those years, but I am grateful to have gotten to know each and every one of them.

After eighteen years in the senate, the day finally came when I wasn't re-elected. One important lesson I had learned as a senator was not to fall in love with the job. I realized that the position belongs to the people, not to me. And since we served two-year terms, I knew that I would be re-evaluated every two years. When I finally didn't get re-elected, I was ready to retire from politics. The night of the election, I went home and slept like a baby. I felt good about the years that I had been in politics and the things I had done.

In my life, I've been blessed in many ways. I've had an interesting life, and if the Lord took me today, I couldn't complain. I've been blessed, and I hope that as I have passed through, I've blessed some folks along the way.

Part II

THOUGHTS ABOUT ISSUES

13. Education

During my tenure in the senate, my primary interest was education. I felt very strongly about the importance of education. Today I feel even more strongly about it because I fully realize that education, as I've often said, is the ultimate emancipator of a society. With an educated society, we are less likely to allow some smart, charismatic individual to come along and develop into a dictator over our country. For this and many other reasons, it is critically important that we educate our society and develop a citizenry made up of individuals who can think independently and responsibly and evaluate issues intelligently.

I think that we've made progress in education, but the question remains: have we made enough progress? If you compare our progress in Georgia to the progress of other states, it's obvious that we have not. It's important that we have a system whereby we can measure our progress and compare ourselves to other states. As a matter of fact, I introduced legislation years ago that required our state to include our children in the NAEP (National Assessment of Educational Progress) testing. Georgia was the first state in the nation that joined that coalition, to mandate legislatively that its students be included in the process of testing. Incidentally, I do not particularly like the term "testing"; I like to use the term "evaluating." Testing has a bad connotation; it seems to be dreaded by everybody, including me. What we are really doing is evaluating the progress of students.

Again, I think it is critically important that we do evaluate the progress of children. If we do not know what kind of progress we are making, if we can't evaluate our students' development, then we don't know where we stand. If we don't have accurate assessments as part of our educational system, we can lull ourselves into a situation such as we experienced in this country back in the Sputnik era, and we don't want to find ourselves having to play "catch up" with another nation that way ever again.

Another reason that I think it's important that we continue to push education is based on a fact that surfaced in some research that I did several years ago. I learned that in the 1930s in the U. S. we had sixty-three people working per retiree, in the '60s it was seventeen people working per retiree, and in the '90s it was three. Now, it's really around one person working. So, we have a social-security problem. I notice that the congress doesn't want to be realistic and deal with this issue, but it had better get moving on it. My point is that we must have full employment in this country, and a solid educational system is critical to full employment. Graduates from our educational institutions must be employable, and the system must be such that it provides people who can support a broad-based economy. We cannot build a stable economy based on just one industry sector. For example, there is great emphasis on service-type industries of late. In my judgment, that is a mistake. Service industries are important, but you can't build a stable economy on them alone.

These are many and varied problems facing our country today. Consequently, it is imperative that we continue to place strong emphasis on producing young people who have had a good basic quality educational experience. From that foundation, they can continue to develop into valuable members of our society.

One mistake that I think we are making today is that we often have a tendency to invest more work and money on the students who do not excel academically as well as we think they should. I understand the logic of that. I don't think we should neglect such students, but the big mistake we are making is implying that because the bright kids can get it, we don't have to place an emphasis on them. I think this is one of the biggest mistakes we are making in public education. We should redirect some of our education dollars and put them towards advanced placement courses for bright students. Those bright students, in my judgment, would bring our SAT testing scores up. Also, some of these bright students are going to be the innovators, the job creators, and the leaders. Consequently, I think we need to pay more attention to the bright students.

When I started in the Georgia senate in 1975, our K-12 budget was slightly over 600 million dollars, if my memory serves me correctly. In 1992 it was 2.8 billion dollars; in 1993 it was 3.1 billion dollars; and now it would be much higher than that. The sad commentary on all this is that we are not making enough progress. For the amount of money that we are spending, we are not making the progress that we should be making.

Now, I'm not going to fault the teachers. As Lester Maddox once said, we could have better prisons if we had better quality prisoners. Well, we could have better schools if we had better quality students. Another important aspect is the curriculum. The educational system should be teaching, in my judgment, those basic core curriculum courses that put us in a situation where we are competent enough to learn on our own initiative.

But the point I want to make is that with all the monies we are spending, we have the same dropout rates, and our test scores have not improved that dramatically. Remediation continues to be a major problem. Now, are we going to be able to eliminate all that? No. The Constitution guarantees us all the right to equal opportunity, but when we are born and are brought into the world, we are not all equal. I wish that I were more equal to some of my friends as far as many capabilities are concerned, but that's just the way it is. The differences between and among individuals are what make families, communities, and nations capable of development, growth, and sustainability. And we have to recognize that, and that's where I go back to this business of being politically correct. Everybody can't learn at the same pace. Yes, we should pay attention to everybody and provide every opportunity.

But it becomes a parental responsibility as well. I've argued for a number of years that somehow or another we need to create parental-responsibility laws so that parents, when they bring children into this world, recognize the fact that if they do not look after those children and show an appropriate interest in raising them, then there are consequences. For instance, if we continue at the current rate of increase in educational expenditures—and I'm not against spending the necessary monies—we may get to the point where we can just about hire an individual to raise every individual born. And when we get in that mode, I think we will have approached our peak in spending. (I make that point simply to say that I think we have to be brutally honest with ourselves and aware of where we are going.)

Another of the things we recognize now is homeschooling. Back when I was in the legislature, I believed that anybody who homeschooled their kids just simply didn't care much about them. I learned, however, that that's the farthest thing from the truth. There are people out there homeschooling their kids for a specific reason: they care deeply about their children. They want to see to it that their children are getting a great academic experience in an environment that meets their parents' standards as far as their social life is concerned. I don't have a problem with that.

As a member of the board of trustees at Piedmont College, I saw the proof that homeschooled students can make excellent college students. When I was looking into that situation, I found that we have lawyers, doctors, teachers, and any number of well-qualified people who want to teach their children at home. I respect that right and think it is important that parents have the right to homeschool their children. These people are accepting, in the deepest sense, the responsibility of rearing their children. Many people want the public schools to do everything for their children, and if something goes wrong they want the schools to accept the responsibility for shortcomings that may properly belong to the family and not the school. That's just wrong.

Another educational issue and one of the realities of life today, is the fact that whether we like it or not, we are living in a society that demonstrates that due to advancing technology, our world is increasingly less confined to our own individual community and language. The ability to communicate in a second language has become more and more important. I think we need to emphasize second languages because the young person who knows how to speak a foreign language is going to have an added advantage. I know there are a lot of people who will argue that if you're coming into America, then you ought to speak English. Well, I don't have a problem with that, but then you also have to be a realist, too. What's happening is that some of those who are coming in aren't learning to speak English, and now we can't communicate easily with them. If we are going to trade with them, we must be able to communicate, and so I think it's important that we place an emphasis on foreign languages.

In Georgia we have a tendency to pass some good legislation that does not get funded. Every governor since 1933 has stated publicly that he would like to see educational improvements in Georgia; that has always been a high priority. During my tenure in the legislature, eleven governors requested that the legislature do surveys and studies to help improve education. And when recommendations were approved into law following a study, none of the eleven governors completed the programs or fully financed them. So, oftentimes, we just give lip service to this process.

I know I'm talking about trying to determine how to hold down costs and spending in education, while at the same time saying we need to fully fund it. I don't know that we can ever afford to fund everything, but on the other hand we've got to budget enough to give the students a quality classroom setting and a quality teacher.

One of the things I like that's happening today is that schools are moving to basic year-round programs. Schools are starting earlier: summer breaks are shorter. This gives teachers more of a break at Christmas and at spring break. Something I like about this trend is the fact that these breaks give students who are not keeping up an opportunity to get in there and work and catch up. And I think that's a very good thing about using this format. There are a lot of good things happening in education, but there are still a lot of things that we need to do to improve.

Georgia's Quality Basic Education (QBE) was a major effort in the area of education. It was, simply, a rewrite of the entire system, of the educational laws in this state. We put in place a whole new funding formula. Now it takes a very good lawyer to understand that formula as it really works, but the point is the legislation and the funding formula as I remember it would have been balanced funding for Georgia's educational system. But what happens is the legislatures—and I'm not blaming the ones today; it happened even in our day—don't really respond regarding full funding. Instead, they fund those items that are most popular, such as pay raises for teachers and for school-bus drivers. I'm not faulting that. But what happens is that when they give those two issues priority, then money for maintenance and operation of school buildings and other costs often are set apart and become the responsibility of the local school systems. The result is that the funding formula is not equal again, and the lawsuits begin. So the legislature can put any kind of funding formula it agrees upon into law, but if it is not funded, it's never going to be balanced. So, lip service is given to this cause, but the plan never really becomes a reality.

There was a lot of support for QBE. It passed the senate unanimously; it passed the house. That happened during the Joe Frank Harris administration. QBE was, again, a rewrite of all the educational laws that existed in the state at that time and was probably one of the most far-reaching rewrites of educational laws. But it was certainly not the only major effort. A lot of people out there are very sincere in their beliefs about education and how to improve education. Having spent so many years involved in various aspects of the education issue, I understand that we've got too many people that seem to know how to resolve all those problems. I've had the privilege of serving on Georgia's State Board of Education, so I've not only been on the legislative side, but I've been on the administrative and policy-making side as well. My opinion is that we probably are meddling too much. That meddling is, of course, especially ineffective when we want certain things accomplished, but have no direction to offer as to how they can be accomplished. We ask for reports, but we don't always really look at them. If I had my druthers, I would take the state superintendent of schools out of politics. I would have that person appointed by the governor and approved by the senate because, whether we like it or not, the reality is that the governor and the legislature drive education. Nevertheless, somehow we need to be very careful that we don't overdo our involvement in the process of education because it becomes a very, very frustrating problem for teachers and administrators. We must remember that, in fact, the system itself is often dragging them down with various requirements and constant changes in priorities.

Another challenge is that a lot of the schools of education don't prepare a teacher properly to teach school. At one point during my tenure in public life, the schools of education were turning out some terrible teachers. Not that they're terrible people, they just weren't prepared. And even now, you have some young people going into the classroom and on the first day of school, they are so frustrated they start crying. I've had beginning teachers tell me things like that, and I'm afraid we're just not making them adequately aware of the real world.

Then again, things have improved. Some of the colleges are doing a much better job than in the past. In my judgment, at one point the University of Georgia had one of the worst schools of education in the state. But I think they've come a long, long way. Now I think they're really doing an excellent job. I think the college with which I was associated, Piedmont College, is doing an absolutely superior job in developing teachers. And there are a lot of other good ones out there. But there are still some that leave students ill-prepared. One of the problems we have in education is we have too many teachers teaching out of their field. We don't need physical-education instructors teaching math if they don't have any math credentials. If you're going to teach math, have a degree in math. Consequently, we need to be more open to specializing, and we need to be more flexible. We might be wise to have processes by which a person can fast track if he or she has a certain amount of academic education and real-world experience to become a teacher. For example, a pharmacist might make a good science teacher because of the basic courses that are part of the pharmacy curriculum and because of the scientific foundation of the profession.

In other words, we need to continue to be aware of the value of a certain flexibility in regards to certification of teachers, particularly in areas of teacher shortage. Another example is that we may need to recruit potential foreign-language teachers from Mexico or from overseas. Currently, we just don't have enough teachers in various disciplines. And I think the situation is going to be even more difficult in the future.

On still another issue, I'm a strong proponent of the early childhood programs. I think they do a good job, and I think that building the basic foundation for the secondary systems is critical. Also, I think we need to encourage and support enrollment of qualified secondary-school students in advanced-placement courses. These courses not only give the qualified students work that engages their minds in ways regular classes might not, but they prepare them for college-level work and may offer college credit.

The challenges are great, but I think we are up to them. We will most likely take the expensive route, but we'll get there. Here is a statement that has inspired me and gives me courage regarding the future of our education system: "From the day your baby is born, you must teach him to do without things. Children today love luxury too much. They have detestable manners, flaunt authority, have no respect for their elders, they no longer rise when their parents and teachers enter the room: what kind of awful creatures will they be when they grow up?" Even though these are the words of Socrates from 399 B.C., they ring true today and have during many other periods of time.

I think we go through cycles. The society of the 60's and 70's was too promiscuous and undisciplined, and I think people have realized that now. Society seems to be moving back to a more thoughtful and far-reaching concern about parental responsibility. More parents seem to be focused on spending quality time with their children and may adjust work and social schedules to accommodate the fact that it is the amount of quality time you spend with a child that counts. Parents need to take significant time to be with their children and work with them. I think that, as a society, we are waking up to that fact and accepting our responsibilities. This is one way we can help ensure a good future for our children and our country.

14. Prisons

It was my privilege during my tenure in the Georgia Senate to be a member of the Georgia Board of Corrections, which was a very interesting experience. In addition, I also served on the legislative committee that dealt with prisons. One major area of concern, in my opinion, has to do with expenditures for prisoners. We spend more per prisoner than we do per pupil. Yes, that is the situation.

We do things in prisons oftentimes that are just asinine, in my opinion; the way we react to things just does not make good sense. This is another area where we want to be so politically correct: we want to be good; we want to be fair. But, I think, on the other hand, we ought to remember that the people who are in prison got there because they violated the rules of society, and, thus, I don't think that they necessarily have a right to certain privileges. I think we ought to love them as human beings, but I think it ought to be what is called "tough love."

I've visited and toured nearly every prison in this state, and I have seen firsthand that prison is not a pleasant place, not a pleasant situation. We are fortunate to employ security people who serve at the prison level. The job they do is absolutely phenomenal, particularly when you consider the amount of pay they get. It seems to me we have more troubles at the top administrative levels of running prisons than we do down at the prison levels. We need to continue to be very, very supportive of and aware of the ills of society and what they are costing us. I think we should certainly try to help the incarcerated work through their problems and try to help them get back out into mainstream society if we can. I don't think we can afford to just incarcerate them and throw away the key. And, yet, we've still got to temper justice with mercy. I used to think that mandatory sentencing was the thing, and I probably supported some of that legislation. But my experiences and observations tell me that there are sometimes extenuating circumstances where mandatory sentences do not serve society well. There are what we might call "innocent offenders," basically well-meaning people who got into situations that led them into behavior contrary to their usual character, but yet they're put in prison for years and years. I knew, personally, of a man who was put into prison for a mandatory number of years—I don't remember the specific facts—but I do remember that before his conviction his wife was very ill, and her situation was affecting him dramatically. His doctor prescribed some medication, drugs that would calm him down and let him accept the awful facts. Well, she died. And he was hooked on those drugs. (The person who told me this story is someone I have a great deal of confidence in.) So the bereaved husband had gone into a store and reached in his pocket to get some money or something. He had a little gun in his pocket, and when he was getting the money out, the gun came out, too, and fell on the floor. Of course, the woman waiting on him panicked, which is easy to understand. He had no intent to harm her, however.

Even though he was not attempting to rob the store or hurt anyone, he was charged and sentenced to many years in prison. Because of cases like this and other generally similar situations, I have just always believed that there are some extenuating circumstances that ought to allow judges a little more leeway in what they do. Now there needs to be uniform sentencing, and I don't know just how you accomplish that, but I can guarantee you—you can get into certain kinds of problems in a rural area, and they'll throw the book at you. But you go to the Atlanta metropolitan areas, and they will put you on probation for a similar problem. It's not fair. I saw that lots of times. Somehow, a fair balance has to be established or else at some point it's going to create a major problem in our society. This is a problem that should have already been addressed. We talk about it, but if you're a politician, you have a tendency to want to speak very harshly regarding crime because if you don't, you will not necessarily get elected. We all are anti-crime, without a doubt. I am. But there are extenuating circumstances. I've seen them. Our laws must be fair. It may not happen often, but if we put even one basically innocent person away, just one person, that's too many.

15. Leadership

One area of concern to me that is changing gears now is leadership. We are in a period of generational shift, so to speak; a lot of the older leaders are beginning to take a back seat, and it is critically important that some new leaders emerge.

We've had a generation of leaders serving in various industry sectors, for example. At one point, leading a big corporation was one of our nation's most prestigious jobs. These corporations were the backbone of our economy. Unfortunately, some of the executives leading some of these corporations have turned out to be crooks. It's just unthinkable! It breaks my heart that we've had some of the very unbelievable things happen, how these leaders exploited the corporations, forgetting that a public corporation belongs to its stockholders, not to its corporate executives.

Consequently, I'm hoping that we will place a lot of emphasis in the future on developing young leaders. We must encourage more and more people to get involved in leadership and to understand the true nature of leadership: that the leader's motivation must center on a desire to make the world a better place and not on personal gain. Furthermore, if you're a good leader, there is sacrifice involved. It's the same as being in politics. It's a sacrifice to be in politics. You don't make money being in politics. I recommend that people who want to go into politics recognize that they are probably not going to make money, and if they do, it may be because, in my opinion, they are doing something crooked. We need to remember the concept of politics as public service. Politicians are nothing more than servants of the people. But we need more and more leaders of that mentality, people that are interested in the cause of humankind.

A lot of people are inspired to go into politics by one issue; they've got one thing on their mind and want to work to make something happen regarding that one issue. However, there are a lot of things on the plate out there. So you cannot focus on just one thing. You have got to be open-minded, and you have got to pay serious attention to a lot of issues. Before you introduce a piece of legislation, you should have researched the issue completely so that you understand all aspects of the issue completely, as well as at the deepest levels why you are doing it and how, specifically, it is going to affect society. Then and only then do you introduce it. Too many bills seem to be introduced based on legislators believing they need to introduce a bill in order to have something with their name on it, something to use in future campaigns and/or as a way to make their mark. All leaders must strive to avoid this temptation.

Something else I think affects the quality of our leadership in legislative politics in Georgia is the fact that legislators have to run every two years. We need to increase the term of legislators from two years to four years. I think it's a tragedy that they have to run every two years. Everybody else in the state is elected for four years. Why in the world do we have our congressmen and our senators all elected for just two years? In practical fact, what happens is they have to concentrate more on being reelected than on being leaders.

Let me turn to two issues in our state that continue to test our leadership, water and roads. We are way, way behind in dealing with water issues. We should have dealt with them years ago. In 1978 I held public hearings all over the state dealing with that issue, bringing the issue to the political leadership and, quite frankly, I didn't get anywhere. Some of the things that we pointed out as possible outcomes of not dealing with the issue then are all now coming true in the worst way. Certainly, it was not one of those issues that you had to be a great visionary person to understand its significance; you just had to have some common, logical horse sense. There is a limit to the numbers of people that certain areas can support. Atlanta, for example, has outgrown its ability to support itself under its own infrastructure, so they reach out and take somebody else's territory and then they take more. They can do it because they've got the political clout. We need to develop restraint in development and growth; we need to recognize the fact that we need to spread the success around.

Planning is critical. Nothing should be done arbitrarily, done without having some major planning process. Knowing, for instance, if you're going to build a road, what kind of development is likely to emerge around that road in twenty or thirty years should be an important part of the design process for that road. Securing adequate right-of-way is a similarly important part of planning for a road.

We cannot just plan for today. We must look twenty, thirty, forty, fifty years ahead. Otherwise we can't afford our system. It takes leadership to ensure the affordability of our system.

I'm a very big proponent of vocational education. A favorite idea of mine regarding that topic is that it is past time for industry and vocational technical education to quit romancing each other and enter into a mature relationship based on real needs and a commitment to a responsible, creative, and productive partnership so that both industry and technical education can attain their mutually rewarding and compatible goals. Again, to make a process like that come to fruition takes leadership.

Another basic characteristic necessary for elected officials—and I remember making statements about this back in the 70's—is the ability to recognize his or her own weaknesses and inabilities. We do not need to wing our way through public decisions on a trial-and-error basis, making errors that prove to be very expensive to the people. Public officials should always use and explore the keen minds and ideas of other people, especially people with strong expertise in the areas for which you are responsible, the people who are qualified to aid public officials in their searches for answers. Public officials should explore the opinions of the public as well. Analyze what you hear; then make decisions.

Ultimately, listening to these groups as appropriate gives a public official a greater chance of shining in the area of public opinion, and, more importantly, of delivering solid judgments that may bring forth wise and exciting new approaches in responding to the needs of mankind. I remember when I was in the legislature that when I was dealing with educational issues, I had the help of about five top, in my opinion, superintendents—I sought advice from other superintendents as well, but there were basically five I would rely on to advise me and give me counsel. Their advice allowed me to be able to make solid decisions on issues that were very important to the educational community. In any aspect of governing, no one can know everything, so leaders must have no fear of seeking input from knowledgeable, qualified people as necessary. Another example from my career comes from the time I was working on the water issues. I surrounded myself with several people that were truly experts in that field. That's how I was able to come to some of the conclusions that I did back in 1978.

One of the things that legislators need is more research people. Universities need to be more involved in providing research data for public officials. You can't make good decisions if you don't have research to back up your data. So often we draft a piece of legislation, and we finish developing it in a room one night about midnight. We're anxious to go home, and when we get home, we haven't any idea how what we have done is going to impact folks. So, the more help we have in terms of research and impact analyses, the better.

In many ways, what I have said regarding leadership in the public sector applies to the private sector as well. We need our leaders in both arenas to have a deep sense of responsibility to those they serve, we need them to be careful stewards of our future in terms of planning, and we need them to surround themselves with knowledgeable, trustworthy, qualified people who can supply them with the necessary facts so that they can make wise and responsible decisions.

16. On Politics

I would like to share with you my personal experiences, feelings, and philosophy about government in an attempt to answer the basic questions of government: What is a politician, and what is politics?

Our opinions of politicians are not very good. Let me share with you some of the better known descriptions of politicians:

> "Politicians are like the bones of a horse's foreshoulder—not a straight one in it."

> "Oaths are tools a politician works with; he may break any oath by his profession."

> "Those who are in politics escaped prison and those who are in prison were on their way to being politicians."

> "Among politicians the esteem of religion is profitable; the principles of it are troublesome."

> And then, the most familiar words of all: "As crooked as a politician."

All my life I have heard and used the expression "as crooked as a politician" to describe any dishonest, corrupt or untrustworthy person. When I first considered seeking elective office, many of my friends urged me *not* to get involved with this "dirty" world lest I, too, would become contaminated in the process. Some of these same friends are now probably sure they were right.

In essence, this demonstrates a common attitude that corruption, compromise, and dishonesty are the rule for politicians, not the exception. And candidly, I must admit that the stories of political corruption beginning with Watergate through Abscam and landing in our own state with the conviction of too many of our own elected state and local politicians give credence to this cynical view of politics and politicians.

However, if this view of politics and the politician being basically corrupt is true, then it must logically follow that we the people of America want our politicians to be corrupt, for, after all, we elect them. And a wise man once said that we get the kind of elected officials we deserve.

Of course, we know that this is **not** a true or realistic view of politics or politicians. Bertrand Russell well said that "without civic morality, communities perish; without personal morality, their survival has no value." Our nation has not survived over 200 years to be the moral, economic, and political hope of the world by having all corrupt elected leaders. Corrupt representatives do not pledge "their lives, their personal fortunes, and their sacred honor" in order to give birth to a nation of great men and women.

The question then is: Why do we so often state a philosophy of politics being a corrupt and corrupting process? The answer in my experience is that we attempt to personalize and categorize politicians in order to simplify our ever increasingly complex and confusing world. We appear to need to view our elected representatives as either totally good or totally evil, as pure saints or unregenerate sinners. We tend to view our elected representatives as *my* representative, not as the representative of all the people. We demand that he act and vote the way we want him to act and vote. In using this personal, simplistic and myopic view, we forget that he was elected to serve all the people, not just *me* and *my* personal views. For there is no way an elected representative can vote and act on the major issues of today without coming into conflict with our individual and personal views.

Let me illustrate this with some very real and personal examples of issues we have faced in the Legislature:

Abortion: Is it a human right of choice for the mother, or is it a form of murder (feticide)?

Alcohol: Should it be a matter of personal choice for adults to drink, or is it a sin?

Sexual Behavior: Is it a personal matter between consenting adults, or should it be regulated by law?

Parimutuel Betting: Is it a realistic and responsible alternative to increasing tax revenues, or is it an immoral activity?

Decriminalization of marijuana. Gun Control. Right to die for persons terminally ill. These examples could go on *ad infinitum, ad nauseam.* The death penalty, prayer in public schools, taxation of church profits and property, welfare, human rights of all kinds, and so on.

So how is an elected representative going to make decisions and vote on such complex and emotionally charged issues without finding himself in opposition to the personal wishes of some of the people he represents? He isn't! He can't! He knows that he must act and vote based on his own philosophy and morality, and attempt to honestly represent the majority view of his constituents.

Those who disagree with his vote will often feel betrayed and angry and will then accuse him of "having sold out to the other side . . . as all politicians do." Is it any wonder that some successful politicians learn to speak in vague generalities, to avoid controversial issues in public and thus seem "to talk out of both sides of their mouths" in order to be re-elected? Or worse, they become demagogues who exploit our human fears, passions, and prejudices and offer simplistic solutions to complex and demanding problems.

If we allow this to continue to happen to us as a people and a nation, we will have become the victims of our own simplistic and unrealistic view of politics and politicians. We will have abdicated our moral, political, and philosophical responsibilities.

As Henry Ward Beecher said from the famous Plymouth pulpit: "Men must choose whether they will govern themselves or be governed." The choice has always been ours in this great Republic. It is still ours today. If we can keep it!

And, on my experience in the Georgia Senate, we have on the whole chosen well those men and women who represent us in the Legislature. I have met some unscrupulous demagogues and a few weak and self-serving representatives, but they are the exception, *not* the rule. My colleagues have usually been professional businessmen and women doing their best to honestly and responsibly serve the people who elected them. Let one elected official do something wrong, and they are all bad. But, let a teacher, businessman, preacher, lawyer, or doctor do something wrong, and it is then an individual issue.

This brings me to my personal view of politics and politicians. The essence of a political philosophy is to see man as the most important end of all human effort and his growth toward responsible freedom as the means to that end. To put it more simply, politics and politicians should have the freedom and growth of man as their chief end. Anything less is a poor, shabby political philosophy which will lead us toward a dictatorship or a welfare state.

We do not want either of these two simplistic impostors as our political reality. We must always insist that man is capable of governing himself creatively and responsibly through elected representatives. We must reject demagoguery and simplistic answers to the complexity that is man and search for responsible freedom. We must reject despair or cynicism when a few people betray our trust.

In closing, let me encourage all of you to demand excellence in yourself and the people you elect. Do not expect them to always vote your way all the time, but do demand that they be open and honest with you in explaining their votes. Do not demand or accept simplistic answers, but do demand realistic and creative ideas to address our problems. Do not demand total perfection from your representatives (God does not run for elective office), but do demand a political philosophy and political actions which reflect a realistic and responsible caring for man's search for freedom.

No, *politics* is not a dirty word. It is the eternal hope and quest of man to live in freedom with grace and dignity. Politics is the blood, bones, and sinews of our nation.

Without a strong, courageous, creative, and responsible political process, all other activities will ultimately have no meaning. Become involved in politics with honesty, caring and wisdom so that the words of Abraham Lincoln's reply to the Minister of Sweden during the Civil War may always be true: "This country, Sir, maintains, and means to maintain the rights of human nature and the capacity of man for self-government."

This is what our forefathers gave us. This is our heritage. May each of us confidently, with God's help, accept it and build upon it as we are involved in the political processes of the people and this nation. For upon our shoulders rest the hope of free people everywhere, that Government "of the people, by the people and for the people shall not perish from the face of the earth."

Part III

POSTSCRIPT

17. My Family and Bobbie

I wrote the previous chapters of this book some years ago, and in looking back at them I decided I wanted to add a more detailed account of my wife, Bobbie, and also of some of my ancestors and other relatives. Although I may have mentioned some parts of their storries already, I hope the reader will indulge me as I speak more completely about them in this postscript.

Bobbie and I met many years ago, probably around 1953 after I graduated from high school. We went to church together at Level Grove Baptist Church. I used to see her at the church and would observe her and the fact that she, in my judgment, would be the perfect catch for someone like me, but I would never have the guts to contact her or speak to her. Anyhow, one day I got a call and was told by a friend of mine that Bobbie would like to meet me. I was absolutely grateful that she would even know me because I never actually talked to her or spoke to her in any way. I very gladly agreed to do it. They got us together, and we rode around together. I was really mesmerized with her. She was a beautiful lady and seemed to be a sweet lady. I asked her if she would go out with me, and she said she would. We set up a date.

I went to pick her up in a ton-and-a-half lumber truck. She wanted to know if it was okay if we would ride in her car. She had a car, but I didn't. I was probably around 18 or 19. For a while after we started dating, she furnished the transportation.

On the first date, I told her I would like to marry her. I didn't ask her would she, but I said I would like to marry her. She, of course, didn't say yes or no, but I'm sure when I said that to her she was sort of shocked that I did. We started dating. We dated for approximately four years, off and on. We dated pretty regularly except when I had to go into the military for two years. While I was in the military, I would write her once a day, sometimes twice a day. When I got out of the service, I had an opportunity to re-enlist, but I told them I would never do that because I wanted to go home to marry the girl I was dating. We dated for quite some time. She never would say yes or no. I understand now why she was hesitant. I didn't have a good job and only a high school diploma, and she was a college graduate teaching school.

I was able to buy a radio station in Sandersville, Georgia, thanks to an uncle of mine, Hershel Webster. I was down there about a year and kept trying to get her to marry me. I begged her to marry me, quite frankly. She wouldn't agree to it for quite some time. One weekend I came up and had sort of made up my mind that she was never going to agree to marry me. I just asked her point blank, "Are you going to marry me or not?" And to my amazement she said, "Yes, I am." Needless to say, that was one of the happiest days of my life.

We were married on March 23, 1958. We had 63 years and 13 days of a wonderful marriage. We both agreed that God definitely put us together. He had to be involved, knowing the situation. At that time I did not know that I was two years younger than she was. I didn't know that until after we had gotten married.

We had two sons. I was madly in love with Bobbie. My entire married life I never had a moment that I was not happy. I look back over the period of time we were married and that was a blessing to have had a wife that I truly enjoyed being married to all those years.

I was already living in Sandersville when we got married. I believe it was an act of God that we were able to build a new home in Sandersville. When we first were married, we lived in an apartment. A friend of mine was developing a subdivision right outside of Sandersville, and I guess you would classify him as a wealthy guy. He told me one day that he would like to have me as his neighbor. I told him that I just could not afford to build a house, I just didn't have the money. He asked me if I was a veteran and I said yes. He told me I could get a veteran's loan and I thought, yes, I could. But I told him that even if I got a loan I didn't have the money to buy a lot. He told me that if I got a loan, he would deed me a lot, and I could pay him back when I could. I took him up on that deal. We built a beautiful little house, and it is still there after many years. Bobbie and I used to go by and look at it. We would pull up in the front yard, and the man that owned it then would recognize us and he'd invite Bobbie to go in and look at it. She was very sentimental about that home. That's the way we got our first home. We lived there for about two to two and half years.

One Saturday night when we were back in Cornelia visiting, I went by to see Jack Bradley, who owned WCON (and I had worked for him at the station). He was a good friend. One day I visited with him in his office in downtown Cornelia when he owned Jack Bradley Insurance Agency, and he asked me if I would like to buy WCON, and I said "Yes, I would." He said, "Well, you let me know by about 9 o'clock this evening if you want it." I don't know why he put that kind of proposal to me, but that's the way it was.

I talked with my Uncle Herschel, who financed my Sandersville station, about it, and he said that it was my decision. I called Jack Bradley back about 9 o'clock that night and told him that I would take it. I told him that I would buy the station, and I had no idea how I would pay for it. I knew that I would have to sell the station in Sandersville to be able to pay for it or borrow a bunch of money, and I didn't want to do that. Anyhow I went back home to Sandersville and called up a friend of mine in Swainsboro, Georgia, a fellow by the name of Johnny Bailes who was a singer with the Bailes Brothers many years ago in country music. He owned and managed a radio station in Swainsboro. I asked him if he was interested in buying the Sandersville radio station, and he thought they might be. He said he and his friends would get together and come over and look at it and let me know. I told him what I wanted for it, and they came over and visited.

At that time I also owned a station in Washington, Georgia, and I was going to try and sell them that one, but they wouldn't take it. But they said they would buy the one in Sandersville. They took me up on my offer and paid me exactly what I wanted for it. That's the way I was able to buy WCON.

The way we were able to build a new house in Cornelia was because when we sold the house in Sandersville, we made about $5,000 on the house. That's where we got our money to build the house we are in today, but it was much smaller then than it is now.

My mother was a Purcell. Her daddy was John Purcell, and I think that is probably how I got the name John. She and my dad ran off to Walhalla, South Carolina, and got married when they were real young. My dad was Haskell Calloway Foster, Jr., and my grandpa Foster was a Senior. I only knew him barely. He died at about age 53. I remember him, but I only remember him being sick. Mom and Dad used to take him food to eat on a Coca Cola tray, and I always thought that Coca Cola tray was so pretty. I never got to know him well. He had an apple orchard, and he also went to Florida and South Georgia to get watermelons and bring them back here to sell. He had some cattle. He was a farmer and farmed in Cornelia on the same road I live on now. I had great grandparents, both paternal and maternal.

One of the reasons I wanted to put a little book together for my grandkids is that I didn't really get to know my grandfather Foster well at all. What I basically know about him is what people told me. I was just too young at that time to even think about what a difference it made.

My Grandpa Foster's wife's name was Kitty Berrong. They lived in Cornelia. They were originally out of Hiawassee in Towns County. My Grandma Foster was married to a Judge Brown the first time and they lived in Gwinnett County until he died. They had three or four children when they were living there. She moved back to Towns County, and that is where she met my grandfather. They got married and lived in Cornelia.

John C. Foster, Sr.

There was Lamar "Bill" Foster, my dad's only full brother. I really liked him. He went to Piedmont College and played football. His half brother was Osbourne Brown, a retired military guy. He had a sister, Allie Ree, who married Herschel Webster. That was my uncle who helped me buy WSNT in Sandersville. There was Pink Brown, a half-brother. He was a very successful minister. I can't think of some of the others right now. My mother had brothers—Walter Purcell, Clarence Purcell, and Clay Purcell—and a sister, Elizabeth Brown. She was married to one of my daddy's half-brothers. There was Mozelle, married to Lester Dover. They lived in Detroit. Clay Purcell also lived in Detroit. He was a car dealer.

I bought my first car from Uncle Clay. I was in the army at that time, and I called him about buying a car. I had accumulated enough money to buy one. I caught a ride from Fort Riley, Kansas, to Detroit. I was coming home on leave. I went to Detroit and bought a Pontiac and Uncle Clay sold it to me real cheap. I got in that Pontiac and drove it all day and all night. I didn't stop until I got down to Athens, Georgia. Bobbie and her sister Betty were down there getting their master's degrees. I went to the dormitory where they were staying, and when I got there Bobbie and Betty were with two cadets or soldiers from the school. That really tore me up. I just turned around and left. She knew I was there. It really was crushing to me. I look back at it and we weren't committed to going steady or anything like that. I was committed to her, but she wasn't committed to me. I can understand why she wasn't committed to me. I was too big a risk.

My Grandpa Purcell was Chief of Police in Cornelia. I didn't really get to know him too well. I liked my grandma a lot, but I wasn't close to them like I am close to my grandkids. One day when I was over there visiting, I was rambling through the house and I found Grandpa's gun. I got it out and was looking at it. It was fascinating to see his gun. He found out I got it. I didn't try to shoot it or anything. I was just looking at it. He took a switch and just gave me a whipping for it. I don't remember how old I was. He gave me a bad whipping. I didn't like him for a long time. Looking back at it, I understand why he did it. I'm not mad at him. I shouldn't have gotten his gun out. I would be upset if one of my young ones had gotten a gun out and was messing with it.

My parents were farmers. Dirt farmers. My father started growing chickens. He was the first chicken grower in Habersham County. He grew for Jesse Jewel. He built this chicken house that was 50 foot long. Now that was a big house! We raised hens and got their eggs. He never would do pullets like they do today. We always had hens. I think the eggs were used for hatching. Then he also bought a sawmill. He sawmilled for a couple of years and was fairly successful. That was how we got a big ton and a half truck that I used for my first date with Bobbie. My mother worked at the sewing plant in Cornelia. She didn't work full time, but pretty much full time. She did that for several years. Their basic livelihood was farming.

My dad would grow hogs, not to sell, but to eat. We would kill four or five hogs every fall. That's a lot of hogs. He would take the meat and salt it down heavy. He would put it in the smokehouse and it was surprising how well the meat kept. We would have about four big lard tubs—I mean they were big, about five gallons each—and my mother would use that lard to cook with. By the time hog-killing season would roll around the next year, that lard would be used up. People say eating all that lard and stuff like that would kill you. My mother lived to be 99 years and 6 months old. It didn't kill her. It was good eating. We were poor as far as money was concerned, but we would always have plenty to eat. Momma and Daddy fed us well. She cooked breakfast for us every morning. We would have biscuits, gravy, fried chicken, and ham. Stuff that I thought was for poor folks. We did well. I could eat five or six biscuits each morning. My dad always said I ate too much; it made me poor to tote it. I didn't gain weight. Not until after I married Bobbie.

John C. Foster, Sr.

My parents always had a big garden. They canned a lot of food. When Bobbie and I got married, we would come home on the weekends, and she would give us some of her canned food. Bobbie's mother would also give us some canned food. We were getting by in Sandersville. She was teaching school in Sandersville. My uncle would never let me pay myself but $60 a week. With Bobbie's salary, we were able to get by pretty well. We had a magnificent life together as husband and wife.

Having a nice house was not a priority for my father. I never did think he could afford one. After I left home, I found out that Daddy had sold the house we lived in and was building a brand new house for my mother. He built it and paid for it. He never had a car. I wanted to go to college, but Daddy couldn't afford to help me. I tried to do it on my own. I went one quarter to North Georgia College. I wasn't prepared for college at all. Daddy didn't care if I went to college. He thought you didn't have to have much education to plow a mule. He envisioned me more as living a life like he did. I was determined that plowing a mule was not to be my lot in life. I didn't want that. I remember thinking how I would love to live in a house with carpet. We lived in a four-room house. It didn't have sheetrock; it had beaver board. That stuff was crooked and warped. When the wind would blow under the house, the linoleum rug would come up. We were really countrified. No restroom. Go outside to use the restroom. No running water. No electricity. My mother would heat up water and put it in a tub in front of the fireplace and that is when we would take our weekly bath. Everyone would use the same water. You wouldn't think about doing things like that today.

I guess it was a good experience. I was thankful for the bath and for the roof over my head. The roof was tin and when it rained you could hear every raindrop. It's hard to believe we never had a television. We had a good radio that was bought from Sears and Roebuck. I was just a poor country boy. My mother and father did buy a house on Pea Ridge, and that was the first house we lived in that had a restroom, a beautiful home that is still there. Living in an environment like that made me thankful for what I had.

Bobbie contributed so much to me. She wanted me to have a college education. When I came out of the military I did go back to college. But I finished college in 1969, and both of my boys were around. I worked full time while I was going back to college. Bobbie could help me with my homework and things like that. She made a major contribution to my education. She was very good in English, and she really would bug me about using the right language. She would correct me a lot, but I never resented it. I always thought God put us together because she was taking a chance on me.

I got a phone call one day from Edgar Cannon, who owned the Habersham Broom Company. He wanted me to come out and visit with him, and I did. He told me he wanted to sell that plant, and he wanted me to buy it. I had never been in a broom plant until that day. I told Mr. Cannon that I had never been in a broom plant until today and that I didn't have any clue or idea on how to run one. He told me he would teach me how to run it. I told him I didn't have the money to buy it, and I wasn't really interested. He told me I didn't have to have the money, that he would finance it. That made me think that if I had the opportunity, I should maybe take advantage of it. So that's what we did. I paid him along as I could.

When I was operating the broom company, I was pretty successful with it. He was always really proud of it. One day I decided I needed to re-do the electrical wiring in that building. It was so old. I had the wiring done, and he came in and noticed that there had been some changes. I thought he might be about to object to what I had done. He wanted to know about it because he told me that he was going to pay for that. That's just the kind of guy he was. I managed to pay him off eventually. We did quite well. There were two or three years I probably made $100,000 a year with it.

John C. Foster, Sr.

I got with Georgia Tech, and they came in and helped set up a system whereby if broom corn went up I would have to raise my price by a certain amount on every broom. It was really a good, unique way we did that. It always made it profitable.

We found out that the business was getting harder and harder. When I went in to the Senate, I turned it over to the guy who worked there for many years. He was basically running a manufacturing operation. I could see the handwriting on the wall. We were trying to sell brooms, and our customers could buy the brooms cheaper than I could make them. They were making the brooms in Mexico and shipping them here. I decided that I had better get rid of this thing. I liquidated it. I was able to sell the accounts and sell the equipment to make the brooms. I kept the property. So that's how I got out of the broom business. It was a smart move.

When I got out of the Senate in 1992, I decided I wanted to do something different. Do something on my own. I started looking around and got with Jerry Boling. We talked about processing paper and making chicken bedding out of it. We got with some folks who helped us get the equipment to do it. We built this plant in the building that I had that would grind up paper. We would mix boric acid in with it and we made bedding for chicken houses. It worked out to be very, very good, but the problem with it was that it cost about twice as much as shavings. Chicken growers couldn't afford it, and I couldn't afford to sell it cheaper. We sold a lot of it. The growers liked it. When they would get rid of their chickens, the chicken houses would be full of bugs. Billions of bugs. But with our stuff, the paper, there would not be any bugs. One load of shavings would be enough for one house, but it would take two loads of paper. Fieldale liked it, and they were big in helping me. They really liked it! They agreed that the chicken growers have to do the best they can to make money.

I made the decision to make a difference in what I was doing, and that is when we started out developing inside insulation for houses. We made cellulose insulation, and I got it approved by the federal government so I could sell it to people to put in their homes. The cellulose is fire-retardant and bug-resistant. They said the only people who could use it would be pest-control people. I started making it, and the plant was doing pretty well. It is still going to this day. It was making money, but the work was hard. I'm not one to sit around in the office and be the boss. I wanted to get out and work. If we had better equipment to make the cellulose, it would not be so hard. I would go home at night, and Bobbie would make me take off my shoes and clothes because I would be so filthy. Bobbie didn't like it. We just decided to get rid of it. I sold that plant, and it was moved to the Stephens-Franklin County line. That plant is operating to this day, six days a week. They are making cellulose insulation. Applegate Insulation is the name.

The company was featured on CNN, and that generated a lot of interest. People couldn't understand why I didn't patent it, and I said I thought it was serving a good cause—it was kind of like the Gospel, and we ought to share it. Cellulose didn't originate with me, but we kind of made it popular. I enjoy the idea of creating something.

While I ran the broom company, I was in the Senate and also ran the paper plant. Bobbie ran the radio station. As always, she did a really good job!

www.ingramcontent.com/pod-product-compliance
Lightning Source LLC
Chambersburg PA
CBHW021344090426
42742CB00008B/740